Copyright Doris Charest

This book belongs to

_____

Scavenger Hunt

This book contains:
- Ideas for you to draw.
- Fun will be had.
- Challenges that will test your skills
- Interesting choices for subject matter
- Find new ways to look at the world
- Develop your skills with every drawing

Find and draw something that starts with the letter N.

Find and draw something that starts with the letter S.

Draw something that is sweet, and you can drink.

Find and draw something that starts with the letter G.

Draw something that the sun can melt.

Draw something that you sleep in.

Draw something that can make music.

Draw something that has no smell.

Draw something that moves and is big.

Draw something that you can travel in.

Draw something that has polka dots.

Find and draw something that starts with the letter P.

Draw something that makes noise when you touch it.

Draw something green that moves.

Draw something that can make moving big boxes easier.

Draw something brown.

Draw something you can read.

Draw something that you can open.

Find and draw something that starts with the letter M.

Draw something that is made of cloth.

Draw something that makes light.

Find and draw something that starts with the letter O.

Draw something that is small and round.

Find and draw something that starts with the letter K.

Draw something that is sweet.

Draw something that is hard and on the ground.

Draw something that smells like an old shoe.

Draw something that can jump.

Find and draw something that starts with the letter H.

Draw something that you find in your pockets.

Find and draw something that starts with the letter T.

Draw something that is fluffy.

Draw something that can move with the wind.

Draw something with fur.

Draw something that moves on water.

Draw something that is small and triangular.

Draw something that you can give to someone you like.

Draw something that floats.

Find and draw something that starts with the letter J.

Draw something that is dirty.

Draw something that you love to watch.

Draw something that you need to cook.

Find and draw something that starts with the letter L.

Draw something that is made of wire.

Draw something easy to kick.

Take a walk. Draw something that you saw on your walk.

Draw something that has stripes.

Draw something that is long and skinny.

Draw something that is fun to lick.

Find and draw something that starts with the letter U.

PRIZE: You are now able to draw just about anything. Give yourself a pat on the back. Celebrate! Completing this exercise book is an accomplishment. Good job!

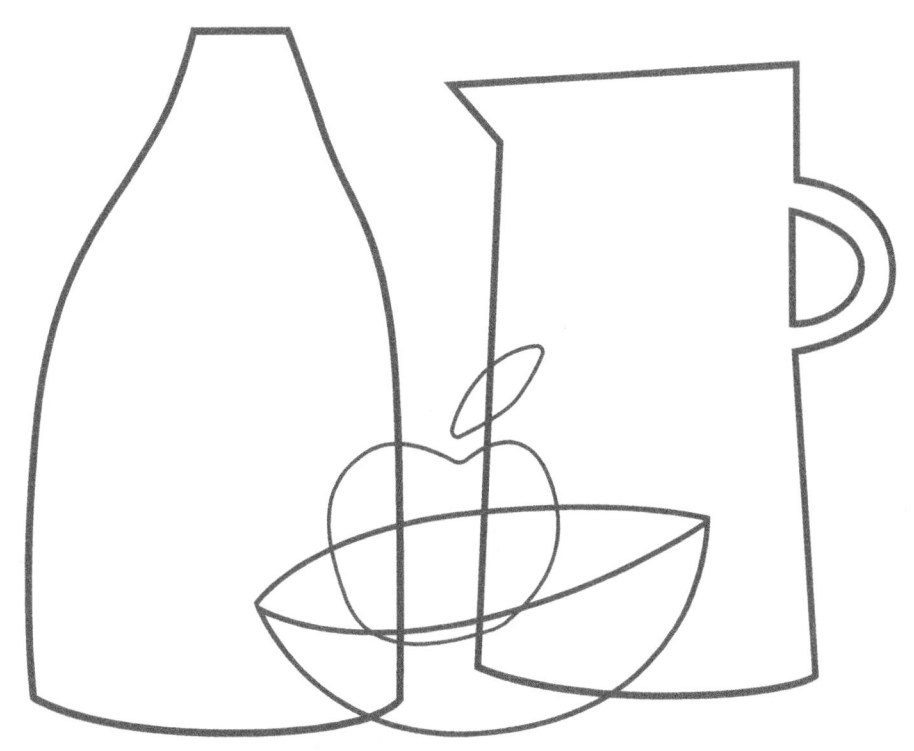

www.ingramcontent.com/pod-product-compliance
Lightning Source LLC
Chambersburg PA
CBHW071123240526
45465CB00023B/787